One Nation one Year

a navajo photographer's
365-day journey into
a world of discovery, life and hope

FEBRUARY 9, 2008   11:05 AM   A snowy but majestic winter morning greets travelers near Leupp, Arizona.

One Nation One Year

a navajo photographer's 365-day journey into a world of discovery, life and hope

photos by
Don James

text by Karyth Becenti
additional editing by Lexi Petronis, Editor-In-Chief of Albuquerque The Magazine

Published by
Rio Grande Books
in collaboration with Albuquerque The Magazine

albuquerque
THE MAGAZINE

Published by Río Grande Books in collaboration with Albuquerque The Magazine
925 Salamanca NW
Los Ranchos, NM 87107-5647
505-344-9382
www.nmsantos.com

Printed in the United States of America

Book and Logo Design: Tom Purtell, Don James, Larryl Lynch

Library of Congress Cataloging-in-Publication Data
James, Don
  One nation, one year / photographs by Don James ; text by Karyth Becenti ; with additional editing by Lexi Petronis.
    p. cm.
  ISBN 978-1-890689-99-5 (pbk.)
 1. Navajo Indians--Pictorial works. 2. Navajo Indians--Biography. 3. Navajo Indians--Social life and customs--Pictorial works. 4. Navajo Nation, Arizona, New Mexico & Utah--Pictorial works. 5. Navajo Nation, Arizona, New Mexico & Utah--Description and travel. 6. James, Don, Jr.--Travel--Navajo Nation, Arizona, New Mexico & Utah. 7. Indian photographers--Southwest, New--Biography. I. Becenti, Karyth. II. Petronis, Lexi. III. Albuquerque (Albuquerque, N.M. : 2004) IV. Title.
  E99.N3J29 2010
  979.1004'972600222--dc22
                    2010005310

TABLE OF CONTENTS

NAVAJO NATION

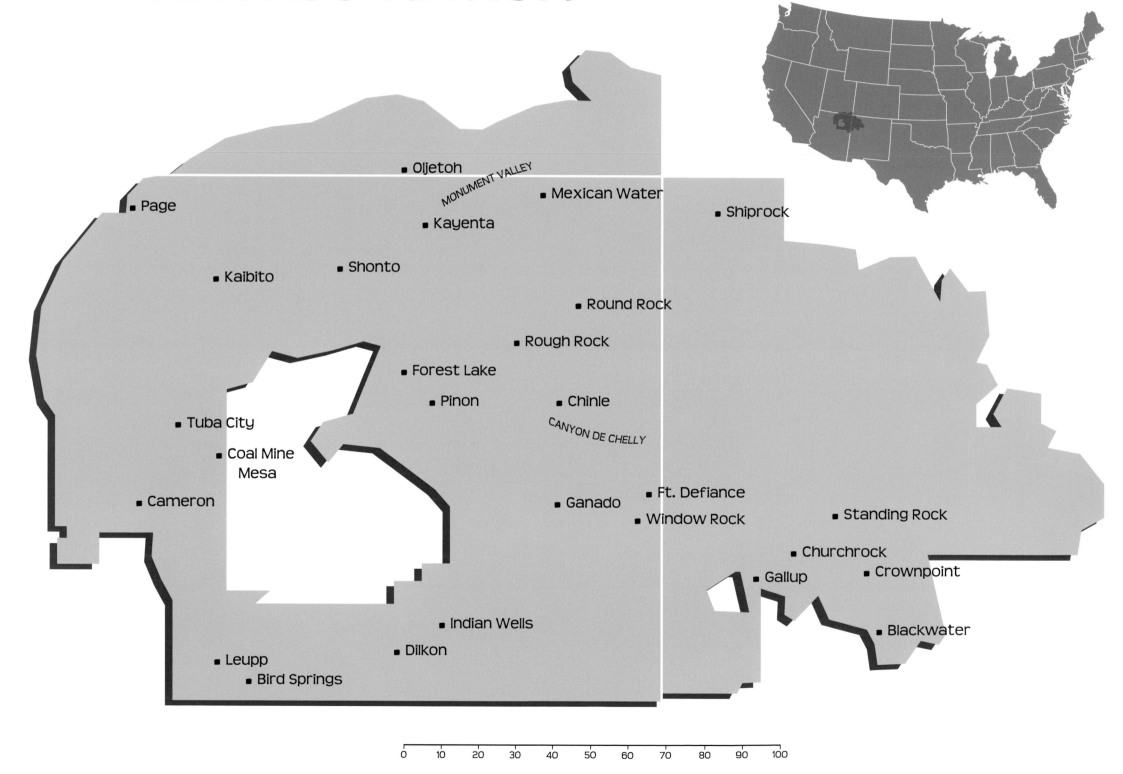

Oljetoh

MONUMENT VALLEY

Mexican Water

Page

Kayenta

Shiprock

Shonto

Kaibito

Round Rock

Rough Rock

Forest Lake

Pinon

Chinle

CANYON DE CHELLY

Tuba City

Coal Mine Mesa

Cameron

Ganado

Ft. Defiance

Window Rock

Standing Rock

Churchrock

Gallup

Crownpoint

Indian Wells

Blackwater

Dilkon

Leupp

Bird Springs

| 0 | 10 | 20 | 30 | 40 | 50 | 60 | 70 | 80 | 90 | 100 |

ONE INCH = 25 MILES

I feel a responsibility to my backyard. I want it to be taken care of and protected."

Annie Leibovitz
World Famous Portrait Photographer

Loliane Tsosie grew up performing physically demanding ranch work in Bowl Canyon, New Mexico. The hard work shows in her hands; her finger was sliced off while mowing in the alfalfa field.

After working as a physician's assistant on the Navajo Reservation for 32 years, she retired to care for her mother, Ilene Braney Tsosie. Loliane is writing a book about her close relationship with her mom.

FEBRUARY 10, 2008   10:32 AM

Lenanuel James (below) and Davon Holiday (right) are long-time friends who traveled to Wheatfields Lake, Arizona, to ice fish for the first time.

The men work for the Navajo Tribal Utility Authority, a tribal enterprise that supplies the people with electricity. They've been friends since they ran cross-country together at nearby Chinle High School.

FEBRUARY 11, 2008   7:13 AM

To the Navajo populace, the mountain Tso Sila,
near Navajo, New Mexico, looks majestically like
a sleeping war chief lying on his back, still wear-
ing his headdress.

FEBRUARY 11, 2008   10:43 AM

In a testament to Navajo artistry and skill, a
colorful wall behind the post office in Window
Rock, Arizona, shows prideful graffiti.

FEBRUARY 11, 2008   7:03 PM

Basketball—or, as it's sometimes called on the Navajo Reservation, rezball"—holds a special spot in families' hearts. Children grow up watching their siblings play high school basketball in front of sold-out crowds.

Here, Miss Navajo Nation Jonathea Tso sings the national anthem before a game between the Window Rock Scouts and the Chinle Wildcats in Chinle, Arizona.

FEBRUARY 11, 2008   7:34 PM

Though the typical high school gym in America seats only a few hundred, Chinle High School's Wildcat Den accommodates several thousand and has the feel of a college arena (note the luxury suites,' pro-style scoreboard and capacity crowd—all for a girls high school game).

FEBRUARY 12, 2008   3:57 PM

In Aneth, Utah, Samuel Jelly has more than enough open land to roam on his bike. He listens to his iPod as he pedals through the vast landscape, just two miles from his house.

FEBRUARY 20, 2008   11:26 AM

Homemade signs like these near Kayenta, Arizona, serve as forms of communication, conveying messages like team spirit, or advertising dates of upcoming country-western dances.

FEBRUARY 20, 2008   2:30 PM

Haven Ute and his family have a foodstand just outside their house in Dennehotso, Arizona. The nearest convenience store is 25 miles away, so Ute does a good amount of business selling snacks.

FEBRUARY 20, 2008   12:52 PM

Hogans are sacred houses for the Navajo people. There are two displayed at Red Mesa Elementary School in Teec Nos Pos, Arizona: the traditional male" hogan (on the left, it has a vestibule at the entrance and is meant for ceremony) and a female" (on the right, with a round top).

FEBRUARY 28, 2008 7:06 PM

Charleston Tso's truck ran out of gas in Chinle,
Arizona. With no money, the military veteran
patiently waits for assistance.

FEBRUARY 29, 2008 3:56 PM

Masani—"grandma" in Navajo—crosses a well-driven dirt road with her sheep. It's common for Navajo shepherds to continue to tend to their flocks daily well into their 70s and 80s.

MARCH 1, 2008 1:36 PM

A deserted sweat lodge sits near Douglas Mesa, Utah. Sweat lodges are used ceremonially by Navajos for spiritual balance, mental cleansing, and physical strength. During the long 'sweats,' people ask Mother Earth for guidance and wisdom.

MARCH 1, 2008 10:19 PM

Billy Crawley II (right), Terrill Redhouse, Chris Katso and Justin Jynison perform with their heavy-metal band, Ethnic De Generation, in Kayenta, Arizona.

Having already opened for major artists such as Soulfly, Otep, and American Head Charge, and logging national and international shows, the band just released its first CD.

MARCH 2, 2008 5:44 PM

James Yellowman (left), Andorra Holly, Parnell Thomas (both below), and Samuel Captian, Jr., ride together as part of the Mossi Riders from Montezuma Creek, Arizona.

The 45 Cat Riders are a group of family, friends, and coworkers who frequently explore the Four Corners area on their motorcycles.

APRIL 2, 2008 4:06 PM

Because cement is scarce on the Navajo Nation, finding a place to practice BMX bike jumping can be a problem. The Navajo Nation Museum in Window Rock, Arizona, provides one of the best places to ride.

(Left) A multi-exposure photo captures Byran Wilson's jumping skill in action.

APRIL 2, 2008 4:32 PM

Byran Wilson, Franklin Cook, Ryan Borchman and Nate Martinez built their bikes specifically so they could compete in BMX-style competitions across the Reservation.

MAY 22, 2008   12:28 PM

In the tradition of old trading posts, the modern convenience store is the place to congregate on Navajoland. Because the land is extremely rural (about 180,000 residents in a Reservation the size of West Virginia), people commonly make one monthly trip to stock up on grocery and household items.

Red Mesa Trading Post in Red Mesa, Arizona is the only spot for miles around to get gas, DVD movie rentals, and other essentials.

JUNE 1, 2008   7:43 PM

Julana Begay of Crownpoint, New Mexico, competes in barrel racing, steer riding, and goat tying in the Indian Junior Rodeo Association. Even during competition, she wears her Navajo hair bun (or *tsi-iyeel*), which is the traditional hair style.

Rodeo is the dominant sport among the Navajo population, both for contestants and spectators. This is likely because the lifestyle of the people is rooted geographically in the cattle and horse culture of the Old West.

JUNE 5, 2008 7:04 PM

A group of buddies from Whippoorwill, Arizona, created a five-hole golf course across the street from their housing complex.

They hammered plastic pipes into the ground to make golf ball cups, flagging them with neon signs so they'd be easier to spot on the rugged, weed-choked terrain.

The group hopes to start a local golf tournament someday. In the meantime, they play only for bragging rights, marking their strokes on a makeshift scorecard.

JUNE 5, 2008 8:34 PM

From left to right: Alex Daw, Alan Begay, Tyson Tsosie, Jeremy Whitehair and Finlee Tsosie.

JUNE 6, 2008 1:28 PM

Jerry Sleuth of Naschitti, New Mexico, taught himself how to stucco buildings when he was just out of high school more than 30 years ago.

Because of the high desert climate, the Navajo Reservation has very cold winters and blistering summers, making versatile stucco the product of choice on most modern home facades.

JUNE 6, 2008   7:07 PM

Patrick Hubbell prepares a teepee for his up-coming blessing of marriage to his bride, An-drea.

Meanwhile, Andrea gets ready for the blessing with the assistance of her mother and grand-mother, who outfit her with silver and tur-quoise barrettes and jewelry.

Patrick and Andrea are students at Arizona State University, where they're studying fine arts and photography.

The Native American Church (NAC) will perform the blessing. The NAC originated with tribes in the Midwest Plains region, and has been prac-ticed across most tribes for centuries.

Navajo Nation President Joe Shirley, Jr. prepares notes on the flight to Kayenta. The position involves plenty of travel, and Shirley often flies to visit some of the 110 chapter houses—or residential districts—of the Navajo Nation.

Shirley checks e-mail on his iPhone as he flies in the Navajo Nation's twin-turbo King Air plane high above the night skies of the Reservation.

JUNE 9, 2008 11:11 PM

At the Red Mesa Chapter House meeting, El-wood and Janette Bigben listen to Navajo Nation president Joe Shirley, Jr. speak about current affairs.

Red Mesa, Arizona, is a small town of 300 near the Utah border. Like many rural communities, governance is conducted by both state and Navajo Nation law. At the heart of most matters is the vast number of homes without running water and/or electricity.

JUNE 11, 2008   8:12 AM

Suzie James lives in a remote mountain home in Klagetoh, Arizona.

At 73 years old, Suzie still looks after her sheep daily in the same way she has all of her life. In the spring and summer, she shears off their winter coats and stores the wool in her shed to sell at market.

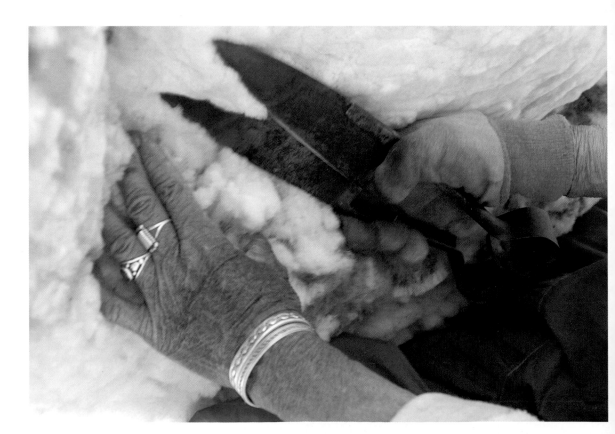

JUNE 12, 2008   4:52 PM

This sewing machine has been an integral part of Gracie Hubbell's life on the Navajo Nation.

She says she gives away the quilts, aprons, potholders and dish towels that she creates because her parents taught her to be generous.

Gracie, who works for the tribal government as a contract analyst, has already started making quilts for her future grandchildren.

JULY 9, 2008   10:07 AM

According to tradition, only females can plant corn—*it needs a woman's touch.* That's Urina Bitcinnie's summer job.

The Navajo Nation's Office of Youth Development in Monument Valley, Utah, creates summer jobs and afterschool programs for teens.

With the money she earns, Urina plans to buy an iPod, so she doesn't have to borrow her friend's anymore.

JULY 11, 2008   8:27 AM

Chelsea and Kobe Holiday saddle their horses for a 30-mile community horseback ride in Douglas Mesa, Utah. The ride takes place every year around the Fourth of July.

Most of the riders are men; women and children set up camp, prep the horses, and cook.

During the ride, Cody Interpreter has his long hair pulled back in the traditional Navajo *tsiiyeel*.

Fern and Carroll Coho have been married for 65 years, and they say they have all they need in their one-room home in Kaibeto, Arizona.

They speak with each other only in Navajo, and were only briefly apart when Fern served in the Vietnam War.

Below is a windmill water holding tank near their house, which is adorned with graffiti that pays homage to war Veterans like Fern.

JULY 18, 2008   12:21 PM

Jack Jones drives 15 miles to fill his tank with water for his home and his livestock, then waits 90 minutes for the tank to fill before heading home.

He lives in a small mobile home in Square Butte, Arizona, where he cares for two horses and a flock of sheep.

JULY 18, 2008 2:01 PM

Johnson Peahson travels to the water pump several times a week. The 20-mile roundtrip results in water for his family, which lives near Black Mesa, Arizona.

JULY 22, 2008 8:18 AM

Nora Montano, Woody Yazzie, and Herman House butcher a sheep for a birthday dinner in Blackwater, New Mexico.

Mutton is a Navajo delicacy, and is part of the daily diet in many households on the Navajo Nation. No part of the sheep goes to waste; even the blood is collected and saved to make blood sausage.

Tenai Lansing becomes a woman during her four-day Navajo coming-of-age ceremony, or *kinaalda.*

Because a traditional round hogan is used for the ceremony, Tenai's father, Tommy Lansing, had to hastily build one outside their modern family home near Cortez, Colorado.

Every morning, Tommy and Tenai's grandmother, Flora Dimitriou, tie her hair back with buckskin.

JULY 25, 2008   9:23 AM

Every morning, Tenai runs to the east to welcome the day. Afterward, she lays on the ground and her father pulls her arms and legs to stretch" her. (Traditionally, a woman performs the stretching; on this day, her father does the honors.)

Later, she performs the stretches on others. She motions her arms over her cousin, from the ground up, which the Navajo diety says will give him height as he grows.

During the ceremony, Tenai is busy: she cooks, dresses in traditional attire, and speaks the Navajo language. The rigorous daily tasks are meant to teach her the work ethic she will need to later become a good wife and mother.

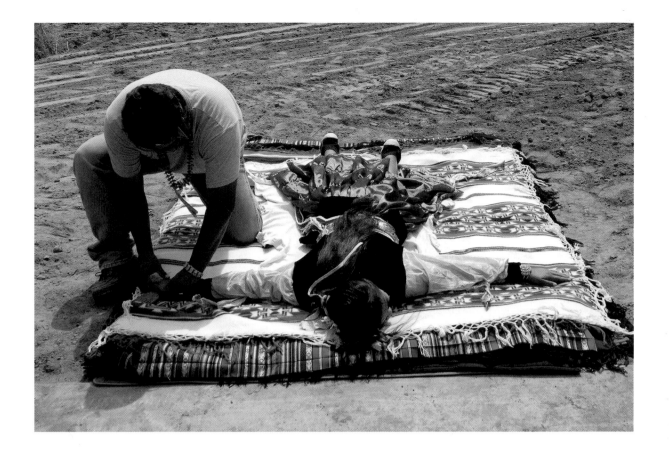

AUGUST 2, 2008   9:05 PM

To celebrate Diné College's 40th year of cultural independence, the main campus in Tsaile, Arizona, held a Battle of the Bands. The fluorescent stage lights up the side of the tallest building on campus.

Diné College offers certificates and associates' degrees, enabling students to transfer to a four-year university. The college has six satellite campuses across the Navajo Nation offering classes, academic advisement, career counseling, and financial aid.

AUGUST 4, 2008   9:16 AM

Bradley and Victoria Blair provide necessities for the people of Lukachukai, Arizona. They own Totsoh Trading Post, where customers not only buy food and supplies, but specialty items such as raw sheep's wool, Navajo wedding baskets, leather strips, cowboy lassos and traditional baby cradle boards.

The Blairs' daughter, Connette, and granddaughter, Daniell, help keep the shelves stocked. The Blair family has owned the store for more than 24 years.

AUGUST 15, 2008   5:34 PM

Cecilia Nez Joe's mother taught her how to weave Navajo wool rugs when she was only seven years old. Now, at age 72, Cecelia works on her rugs mostly in her spare time in her hometown of Gold Springs, Arizona.

AUGUST 15, 2008   8:01 PM

The sun sets over the Navajo Nation in Steamboat, Arizona.

AUGUST 16, 2008   12:23 PM

The Long family (L to R: Paul, Sr., Paul, Jr.; Paul-son and Carlos) loves softball. They host an annual tournament each year in Rock Springs, New Mexico, and use the proceeds to buy school supplies for local elementary students.

SEPTEMBER 3, 2008   7:53 PM

Jerrick Hildreth, from Coolidge, New Mexico, is a
24-year-old saddle bronc rider who competes
in rodeos across the Navajo Nation.

Rodeos are known to have high injury rates,
but many young Navajo men live for the adren-
aline rush that comes from going up against
thousand-pound animals.

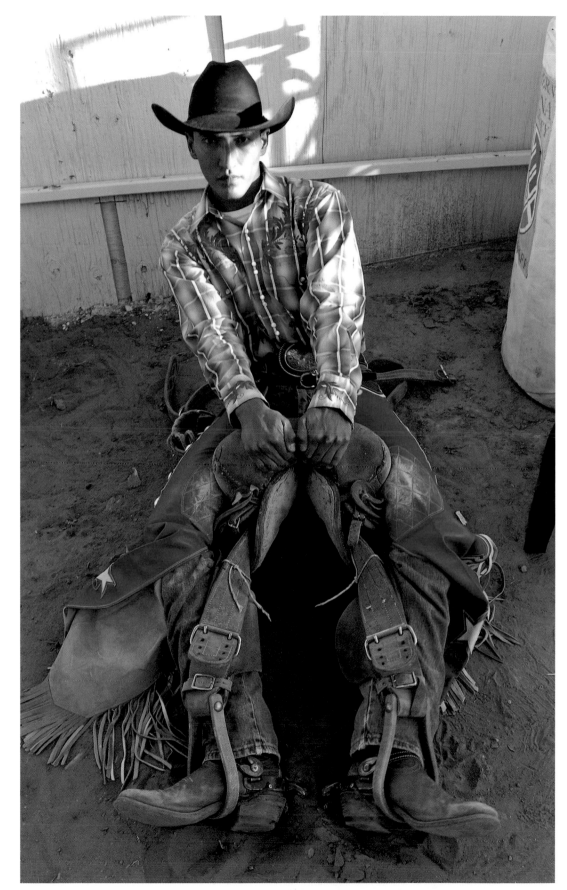

SEPTEMBER 4, 2008 5:16 PM

When Jonathea Tso was crowned Miss Navajo Nation, people gave her gifts to wear on her yellow sash: a turquoise cornstalk pin from her aunt, a star pin from a deputy in Apache County, and even a Superbowl pin.

The competition for Miss Navajo Nation is intense. It takes place at the annual Navajo Nation Fair in Window Rock, Arizona, and contestants are quizzed in the Navajo language, must butcher a sheep, and demonstrate a contemporary talent, among other things.

SEPTEMBER 4, 2008 5:02 PM

As Miss Navajo Nation 2007-08, Jonathea had a responsibility to keep up customs and the Navajo language. She compares her hard work to the ritual of the *kinaalda* ceremony—she says it's like performing the four-day ritual for the entire year. At right she poses with her grandmother, Mae N. John, who Jonathea says has been her role model.

SEPTEMBER 6, 2008 10:49 PM

During the 2008 Miss Navajo Nation competition, Jonathea passed the crown to Yolanda Charley. Yolanda reigns for the 2008-09 year, and will take her position seriously—she plans to visit all 110 chapter houses within the Navajo Nation in order to reach out to the community.

SEPTEMBER 24, 2008   12:23 PM

Hay for livestock is always in demand on the
Reservation, even if you don't have the easiest
means to transport the bales home.

SEPTEMBER 27, 2008   8:12 PM

Milayia and Lionel Yoe prepare to get married in the traditional Navajo way. Before Milayia enters the hogan in which the marriage will take place, she covers her head in a blanket. She will be concealed until Lionel calls for her during the ceremony.

After the wedding, the couple plans to build their family home in Lionel's hometown of Rough Rock, Arizona.

SEPTEMBER 29, 2008   4:29 PM

Alena Sayitsey works at the Monument Valley Navajo Tribal Park in Arizona, where she meets people from all over the world who come to see and photograph the wind-carved sandstone columns that spread across the park's 140 square miles.

Picture-taking is also in Alena's future; she has plans to own a photography studio, where she will take school and family portraits.

OCTOBER 1, 2008 7:22 PM

Elise Salt makes tortillas on an open-fire grill, a staple of Navajo outdoor cooking that utilizes only flour, water, baking powder, salt and lard.

Elise and other women set up an overnight camp for riders who took part in a community horseback trip from Kayenta, Arizona, to Shiprock, New Mexico.

In the foreground at left are cubes of canned meat, which is very popular on the Reservation because it doesn't need refrigeration.

OCTOBER 2, 2008 8:08 PM

The crew and riders sing and talk into the night, keeping each other company around the campfire.

NOVEMBER 30, 2008   3:25 PM

Pete Gilmore believes that boxing teaches hard work, dedication, and courage. The former boxing champion and Army specialist—he spent time as a combat medic in Iraq—started a boxing program in Kayenta, Arizona.

He's also taking online classes through Northern Arizona University to earn his bachelors degree. He says he may become a teacher.

Derrick Begay is the first Navajo cowboy to qualify for the National Finals Rodeo. Derrick grew up around livestock and has been a life-long rodeo competitor (he learned from his dad, who was also on the rodeo circuit). Living the rodeo life means that he spends eight months a year traveling and competing.

Below are Derrick's NFR official contestant number (which is pinned to his shirt during competition) and his parking pass to the Thomas & Mack Center, site of the championships.

DECEMBER 31, 2008   8:55 PM

New Year's Eve is a special time for celebration. At the Navajo Nation Museum in Window Rock, Arizona, people play Navajo string games, which according to tradition should only be played during the winter months.

The object is to create objects and shapes using nothing but your fingers and a piece of string.

JANUARY 1, 2009   12:01 AM

Fireworks shimmer over Window Rock, Arizona, as part of the New Year's Eve festivities.

JANUARY 10, 2009   1:43 PM

Kyle Carillo shoots photos for a calendar of Native American women near Kayenta, Arizona. The high school senior plans to attend Mesa Community College in suburban Phoenix, Arizona, and major in photography and graphic arts.

Kyle says his ultimate goal is to photograph for fashion magazines such as *Vogue*.

JANUARY 11, 2009 4:15 PM

Eugene Chee, Sr., is a pastor in Oljeto, Utah. He gives sermons in Navajo at the Oljeto United Methodist Church. He also plays harmonica and guitar at the local nursing home to raise people's spirits.

When he's not preaching, he tends to his flock of sheep.

Derrick Terry, Gordon Isaac, and Tony Skrelu-
nas started a business together, Kenya Earth:
A Sustainable Development Firm, near St. Mi-
chaels, Arizona.

The trio of Navajos consults with clients about
introducing environmentally-friendly technol-
ogy and alternative energy to the Southwest.

JANUARY 18, 2009   6:35 PM

Walter Hunter, Roy Ramone and Bobby Mariano are members of the Navajo country band Full Diamond, which formed in 2003 in Prewitt, New Mexico.

Chapter houses, recreational centers and school gyms across the Reservation are popular venues for country dances on weekend nights.

JANUARY 19, 2009   11:36 AM

Joe Vandever, Sr. became an important part of American history in 1943 when he was called to serve as a Navajo Code Talker in the U.S. Marines during World War II. He was barely 20 years old at the time.

The Code Talkers were widely credited with providing unbreakable codes that baffled the Japanese, resulting in a swift victory for American forces. At left is a photo of Vandever translating codes in the Pacific theater.

Today Vandever lives in Haystack, New Mexico, with Bessie, his wife of 63 years, and travels to promotional appearances with other celebrated Navajo Code Talkers.

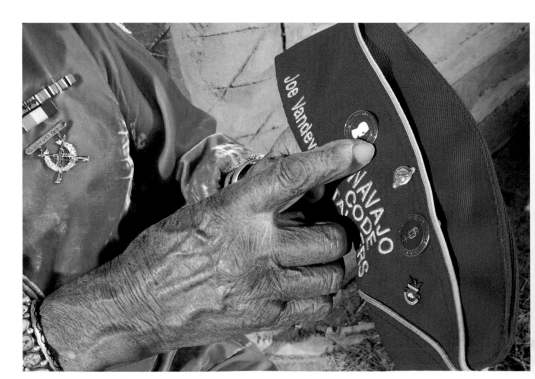

JANUARY 21, 2009   8:27 AM

A pick-up truck sits in a Window Rock, Arizona, parking lot, loaded with freshly cut firewood from a Navajo forest.

A large number of homes on the Reservation are heated with wood stoves, and a common sight in winter is the roadside sale of cut fire-wood (typically $60-100 for a pick-up load).

JANUARY 26, 2009   1:31 PM

At the Navajo Nation Council Chambers in Win-dow Rock, Arizona, council delegates debate the problems of the Navajo Nation and work together to find solutions.

Though there are 88 council delegates repre-senting 110 Navajo chapters, there is a discus-sion underway to reduce the number of coun-cilmen to 24.

JANUARY 26, 2009   3:21 PM

Nathanael Sells trained hard to join the Navajo Nation Fire Department. On his first firefighter call, he helped support the water hose and was on standby for CPR and first aid.

He's planning on attending the University of New Mexico branch in Gallup, New Mexico, so that he can become a paramedic and move to a bigger department in a larger city.

At right is the department's official seal. Note the use of arrowheads, similar to the Navajo tribal seal.

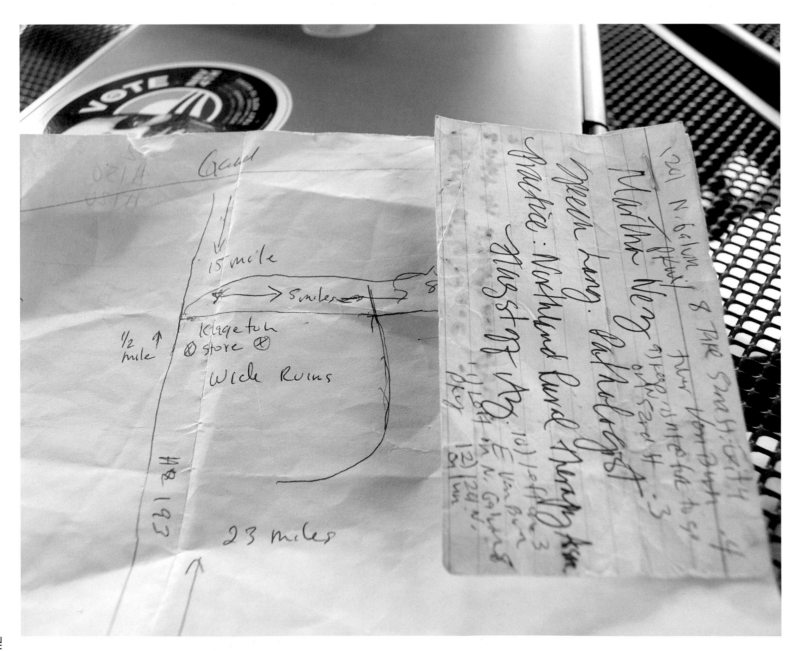

JANUARY 27, 2009   3:54 PM

Natasha Kaye Johnson is a freelance writer, actress, and a legislative staff assistant at the Navajo Tribal Council Office of the Speaker.

Natasha, who's from Twin Lakes, New Mexico, has been published in the *Navajo Times*, *Gallup Independent*, *Tribal College Journal*, and *New Mexico Magazine*, in addition to several Web sites. She's also writing a children's book.

JANUARY 28, 2009 10:40 PM

As comedians, Ernest David Tsosie III and James Junes make people laugh for a living. They travel across the Navajo Nation with their act, which reflects the humorous side of the Navajo people. Here they entertain a crowd of a few dozen people at the Community Center in Chinle, Arizona.

They even use props—like this paddle from their boarding school days. The duo hopes to promote a healthy lifestyle, bringing awareness to alcohol, drugs, and domestic violence problems.

It is said that the first Navajo woman gave the tribe four sacred mountains, to indicate where the people would live.

It's within the boundaries of these four sacred mountains that the Navajo Nation thrives today.

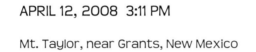

APRIL 12, 2008 3:11 PM

Mt. Taylor, near Grants, New Mexico

MARCH 3, 2008 6:09 PM

San Francisco Peak,
near Flagstaff, Arizona.

JANUARY 31, 2009 5:03 PM

Hesperus Peak, in the San Juan
Mountains, Colorado

FEBRUARY 2, 2009 1:47 PM

Blanca Peak, in San Luis Valley, Colorado

In traditional Navajo teachings, The Holy People instructed First Man and First Woman on how to build hogans (sacred buildings).

The first hogan, of the "male" type, was made for ceremonial purposes; the "female" hogan was built for families to live in.

Hogans are still embraced for ceremonial and residential use across the Navajo Nation. And as the following examples show, hogans are made with numerous different materials, and variations on the round theme.

One thing remains constant, however: doorways of all hogans must face east, toward the rising sun. It's believed that good things come from the east. Navajos welcome the new day and pray eastward, with corn pollen.

Teec Nos Pos, Ariz

Black Water, N.M.

Rough Rock, Ari

Ventana Mesa, Ariz.

Monument Valley, Ariz.

Monument Valley, Ariz.

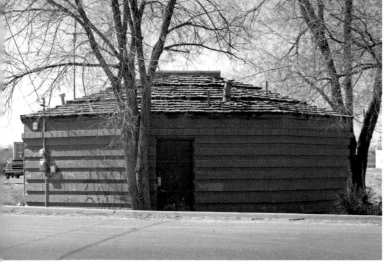

Shiprock, N.M.

Wheatfields, Ariz.

Forrest Lake, Ariz.

Pinon, Ariz.

Coal Mine Mesa, Ariz.

Coal Mine Mesa, Ariz.

Gap, Ariz.

Gold Springs, Ariz.

Seba Delkai, Ari

Willow Springs, Ariz.

Willow Springs, Ariz.

Willow Springs, Ari

Gap, Ariz.

Gap, Ariz.

Inscription House, Ar

Kaibito, Ariz.

Tonalea, Ariz.

Kaibito, Ariz.

Kaibito, Ariz.

Kaibito, Ariz.

Cameron, Ariz.

Montezuma Creek, Utah

Ismay, Utah

Hard Rocks, Ariz.

Hard Rocks, Ariz.

Forrest Lake, Ariz.

Sand Springs, Ariz.

Dinnebito, Ariz.

Dinnebito, Ariz.

White Horse, N.M.

Estrella, N.M.

Star Lake, N.M.

Chaco, N.M.

Blue Canyon, Ariz.

Blue Canyon, Ariz.

Chinle, Ariz.

Klagetoh, Ariz.

Sawmill, Ariz.

Kinlichee, Ariz.

Many Farms, Ariz.

Many Farms, Ariz.

Greasewood, Ariz.

Red Mesa, Ariz.

Oljeto, Utah

Alamo, N.M.

Teec Nos Pos, Ariz.

Mystery Valley, Ariz.

Dilkon, Ariz.

Church Rock, Ariz.

Hogback, N.M.

Rough Rock, Ariz.

Tohajiilee, N.M.

Dilkon, Ariz.

Black Water, N.M.

Oak Springs, Ariz.

Chilchinbito, Ariz.

BlackWater, N.M.

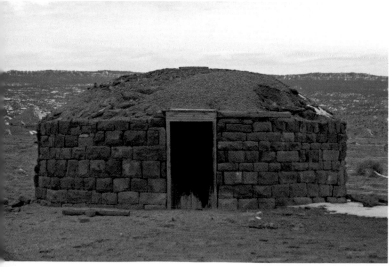

Naschitti, N.M.

Seba Delkai, Ariz.

Castle Butte, Ariz.

FEBRUARY 4, 2009 4:28 PM

A sign near Shiprock, New Mexico,
bids visitors goodbye.

Don James

From the first time I picked up a camera in high school, I have always dreamt about exploring the relationship between my love of photography and my Navajo culture. The idea of photographing Native Americans has been around since the invention of the camera but most photos have been through the eyes of non-Natives.

Plenty of books have been published about Navajos but none quite the way I wished—which is Navajos, raised on the reservation from birth, photographing fellow Navajos.

After people graduate from college they often travel to a foreign country to learn more about the world and other cultures but I wanted to further explore my own culture and country first. I figure it's more important to deeply know where I am from before I know more about other people.

That's how the idea for this book was born, from a need to tell our own story. Being Navajo gives me the ability to blend in with my people, to see past the stereotypes, and to celebrate the ways we define ourselves. Just a few weeks after outlining this project, I decided to hit the road with nothing but the bare essentials—and my Nikon camera.

After my grandpa died I learned never to let an opportunity pass by me. His death was a wake-up call. One morning I had planned to visit him, but for some unimportant reason I didn't—and that night he passed away. From that point on, I decided if I was going to do anything, I would just do it. So when the opportunity came to travel and photograph the Navajo Nation, to make my dream come true, I seized the moment. Thanks, *cheii*.

I was living on $100 a week, sleeping in my truck, showering whenever I could (about twice a week), worrying about people not accepting my camera. But living like a poor man was just fine because I was also living a dream. My journey became more important to me than anything else in life. I learned to be humble toward my people, and frugal with my money. I learned more of my Navajo language, and how important it is to respect my culture. I learned to appreciate my family, and I learned that happiness comes in many different forms. What mattered most was being able to do what I love.

On my journey I met the most amazing people—people I wouldn't otherwise have come to know. I took it as though everyone I met during those 365 days was because I was supposed to meet him or her. They crossed my path because fate allowed it.

Karyth Becenti

I live for writing. I have loved the play on words from the time my mother read me children's books. I grew up to be a writer and graduated with my bachelor's degree in English, majoring in professional writing from the University of New Mexico in Albuquerque, New Mexico. I'm from the Navajo Nation, born and raised in Crownpoint, New Mexico, where the Navajo culture continues to flourish.

My appreciation for the written word also comes from professors who pressed me onward. The challenge pulled me in and it has not let me go—I won't let it.

In search of my next challenge, this project was presented to me and I took the opportunity to write. Not only would I be writing about Navajos but also stepping deeper into the life I knew growing up. I can relate to and understand what it means to drive two hours to experience restaurant dining, or play in the dirt as a child with grandmother's old cooking pans. Each Navajo family has its own ways of living and surviving on the Navajo Nation, and through this project I wanted to see how someone's day went from the other side of the reservation.

As this photo book unfolded, I saw the lives of Navajos in Utah and Arizona. They do exactly what I was exposed to growing up, which is the love of activities like basketball and rodeo. The *kinaalda* ceremony, which I went through as a young girl, was something that almost every family held high. Most importantly, it was clear the love of the Navajo culture is still intact.

I also met people who inspired me, like women who engaged themselves in demanding physical work while raising their family or taking care of their parents. And I am still intrigued by the fascination of rodeo—anything that deals with the interaction between humans and any animal larger than a Great Dane is captivating!

In the end, I am pleased to see that a lifestyle I grew up with continues to prosper. During my travels to interview some of this book's subjects, I was very happy to hear that the Navajo language is strong and still important. I also found my heart will always be in the Navajo Nation, alongside with my love of writing.